GOODNESS and MERCY MINISTRIES

Church According To Bible (CATB)

Pastor Kelvin McGee

Copyright © 2016 by Kelvin McGee
All rights reserved
Printed and Bound in the United States of America

Professional Publishing House
1425 W. Manchester Ave. Ste B
Los Angeles, California 90047
Telephone: 323-750-3592
Email: professionalpublishinghouse@yahoo.com
www.Professionalpublishinghouse.com

978-0-9983089-3-7

First printing December 2016

No part of this book may be reproduced, stored in a retrieval system or transmitted in any form or by any means without the prior written permission of the publisher—except by a reviewer who may quote brief passages in a review to be printed in a newspaper, magazine or journal.

For inquiries contact: operationcut@yahoo.com

Table Of Contents

Mission Statement 5

The Symbolism of the Cover 7

Introduction 13

Doctrine of Deity 17

Not Trinitarian: God-Headtology 31

Doctrine of Man 39

Doctrine of Role-ship 55

Doctrine of Presentation and Socialization 65

Doctrine of Fine Arts, Entertainment, and Fellowship 77

Conclusion- The Affirmation 83

Mission Statement for the Goodness and Mercy Ministries

"Our primary objective is to be the church that focuses on love, forgiveness, a new start, and empowerment through Christ Jesus."-II Corinthians 5:17. We endeavor to preach and present the gospel that will assist one in discovering, and re-directing their positioning in life to align up and stay with God's plan.

The Symbolism of The Front Cover

The Holy Bible- represents the word of God. C.A.T.B. *(Church According to Bible)* endeavors to teach the word of God in its fullness. When we as believers in Christ obey his word with our whole heart, we will be effective in every area of our lives. God's word will bring:

The Green Leaves – (Growth and Abundant Life)

Green is primarily associated with plant life. As a result, we can view it as a symbol of natural growth and life. The exception is its use in Leviticus to denote disease which shows our frailty without God.

Direct Meaning:

- Describes a meat offering - Leviticus 2:14
- Describes edible plants - Genesis 1:30; 9:3, II Kings 19:26, Job 39:8, Psalm 37:2
- Trees - Exodus 10:15, Deuteronomy 12:2, I Kings 14:23, 2 Kings 16:4; 17:10, II Chronicles 28:4, Psalm 37:35; 52:8, Isaiah 37:27, Jeremiah 2:20

Opposite Meaning:

- Disease - Leviticus 13:49; 14:37

Color Symbolism:

- Rest - Psalm 23:2

  Life - Isaiah 15:6, Psalm 23:2, Ezekiel 17:24, Luke 23:31
- Growth - Ezekiel 17:24
- Fruitful - Jeremiah 11:16; 17:8, Hosea 14:8, Luke 23:31
- Fresh / undefiled - Song of Solomon 1:16, Luke 23:31
- Maturity - Job 15:31-32
- Frailty - Psalm 37:2

Associated Symbols:

- Grass - *man / flesh* (Psalm 37:1-2; 92:7; Revelation 8:7, I Peter 1:24, Isaiah 40:6-8; 51:12), *weakness* (Psalm 102:4; 102:11, Revelation 8:7), and *growth* (Psalm 72:16; 92:7, Job 5:25)
- Trees - *coverage* (Psalm 37:35), *trust* (Psalm 52:8), *man* (Matthew 3:10; 7:15-18, Mark 8:24), *and the Cross* (Acts 5:30, I Peter 2:24)

The Purple Sage – (Royal Priesthood-Peculiar People) – 1 Peter 1:14-15; 2:9

The Symbolism of the Cover

Along with **blue**, **scarlet**, and **crimson**, purple is used to describe hangings and fine materials. The dye was extracted from a particularly scarce family of shellfish which made it quite valuable. Purple became a symbol of royalty and riches due to the scarcity of its dye. When examining the associated symbols we see that purple relates to righteousness, kingship, outward show, virginity, separation, hidden, the heavens and habitations.

Direct Meaning:

- Describes hangings, curtains, and coverings (along with **blue** and **scarlet** / **crimson**) - Exodus 26:1;36; 27:16; 28:8, II Chronicles 3:14; etc.

- Fine materials - Numbers 4:13, Judges 8:26, Proverbs 31:22, Luke 16:19, Revelation 17:4

- Describes the dying trade - II Chronicles 2:7, Ezekiel 27:16, Acts 16:14, Revelation 18:12

Opposite Meaning:

- Royalty, but in mockery - Mark 15:17;20, John 19:2;5

Color Symbolism:

- Royalty - Judges 8:26

- Riches – Proverbs 10:22, Revelation 18:16, Luke 16:19

- Corruption of riches - Revelation 17:4

Associated Symbols:

- Robes - *righteousness / righteous judgment* (Job 29:14, Isaiah 61:10, Luke 15:22, Revelation 6:11; 7:9;14), *kingship* (I Kings 22:10; 30-33, I Chronicles 15:27, Isaiah 22:21, Jonah 3:6), *outward show* (Luke 20:46), and *virginity* (II Samuel 13:18-19)

- Curtains - *separation / hidden* (II Samuel 7:2, I Chronicles 17:1), *the heavens* (Psalm 104:2, Isaiah 40:60), and *habitations* (Isaiah 54:2, Jeremiah 4:20; 10:20, Habakkuk 3:7)

MORE ON "PECULIAR"

"Peculiar" (in the Greek) means one's own such as property, or privilege belonging exclusively or characteristically to a person." 1 Peter 2:9 and Titus 2:14 say essentially the same thing. The word *"peculiar"* can refer to "property" in the Greek but is defined in its adjective form as "unique", "unusual", distinctive and "special". So, if we spell it out, we are God's property who is special and unique! Isn't that something that God imparts a word that acts as both a noun and an adjective in a complete sentence.

The Blue Sea –

Blue is used quite extensively in the Old Testament to describe the various hangings in the holy places. It is also used as a symbol of wealth and the corruptions thereof, but it should be noted that purple is used far more frequently for such distinctions. In general, blue should be viewed as a heavenly color. When looking at the endless ocean on the front, we must bear in mind that water (as noted in the associated symbols) refers to the spirit. (John 4:13-14, John 7:38) Blue was one of the gemstones that was encased within the breast plate of the priest. This connects it spiritually to righteousness (Ephesians 6:14).

Direct Meaning:

- Describes hangings, curtains, coverings (along with **purple** and **scarlet / crimson**) - Exodus 26:1;36; 27:16; 28:8, II Chronicles 3:14; etc.

- Holy covering - Exodus 28:31, Numbers 4:5-7;11-12, Esther 8:15

- The Lord's commandments - Numbers 15:38-40

Opposite Meaning:

- Corruption through vanity, whoredom and idolatry - Jeremiah 10:8-9, Ezekiel 23:3-8

Color Symbolism:

- Heavenly - Exodus 24:10, Ezekiel 1:26; 10:1 (sapphire)

- Holy service - Exodus 28:31, Esther 8:15

- Chastening - Proverbs 20:30 (KJV)

Associated Symbols:

Water(s) - *spirit* (John 4:13-14; 7:37-39, Revelation 21:6; 22:17, Matthew 3:11-16), and *people / multitudes* (Revelation 17:15, Jeremiah 46:7-8; 47:1-3, Isaiah 8:7; 17:13)

(Most of this section is extracted from the website: "Riding the Beast.com". The section is entitled: "Color Symbolism and Color Meaning in The Bible.")

INTRODUCTION

At Goodness and Mercy Ministries, C.A.T.B. we believe there are 2 major components that builds a solid church body, and develops a productive individual. The components are as follows:

    I. <u>**One's Spiritual Belief System**</u>—This is the spiritual belief by which ones places total faith in God to guide them throughout life, while fulfilling their purpose. Our spiritual belief is in:

A. The Doctrine of Deity

- This consist of the Godhead—God the Father, God the Son, and God the Holy Spirit

II. Knowing Why We Were Created—Knowing why we were created leads us to who created us, the practices needed to stay in complete awareness and respect of the creator.

A. The Doctrine of Man.
B. Not Trinitarian
C. The Doctrine of Roleship.
D. The Doctrine of Presentation
E. The Doctrine of Fine Arts

THE DOCTRINE OF DEITY

THE DOCTRINE OF DEITY

I. <u>GOD THE FATHER</u> *(Theology)*

We believe that God is the supreme authority of the God-Head and everything done according to scripture was done according to His will and divine command. We believe He is the creator of mankind and we are made in His image and likeness. It is to him that we pray to through His son Jesus Christ (John 14:6). It is in and by Him that our purpose is established.

<u>Scriptures that confirm this belief are:</u>

- **2 Timothy 3:16-17**
  King James Version (KJV)

  All scripture is given by inspiration of God, and is profitable for doctrine, for reproof, for correction, for instruction in righteousness:

  That the man of God may be perfect, thoroughly furnished unto all good works.

- **Philippians 1:6**
  King James Version (KJV)

  Being confident of this very thing, that He (God) which hath begun a good work in you will perform it until the day of Jesus Christ:

- **Proverbs 16:3**
  (*King James Version -KJV***)**

  Commit thy works unto the LORD, and thy thoughts shall be established.

We believe He is omnipotent, omnipresent and the only one who is omniscience *(all knowing)*. We believe there is no one more greater, more merciful, more loving, longsuffering, and mightier than God the Father (Lamentations 3:22 – 3:23, 2 Peter 3:9, Luke 6:36,1 John 4:8).

We believe the interactive relationship with God the Father is conditional and not unconditional *(Genesis 6:5-6, Psalm 37:4; Proverbs 6:16-19,16:3; John 14:15; James 4:8, Romans 1:28)*. We believe His love is not unconditional as most people have taught throughout the ages but it is constant and enduring (Deuteronomy 7:9, Psalm 100:5, Lamentations 3:22 – 3:23, Romans 5:8). Many scriptures show us that there are some things that God does hate *(Proverbs 6:16-19; Psalm 5:5). The Hebrew word is* אנש *sane' which literally means to hate.*

We believe in the assigned names and the redemptive names of God that are assigned to Him and used to approve Him in scripture.

Assigned Names by God:

- **I AM THAT I AM** – Exodus 3:14- Jehovah-God is everything of importance be it in the past, present, or future. He is I am, I Was, and I Shall Be. To make it plainer, one can say of Jehovah that "I Am Now, I Always Was, and I Always Shall Be.

- **The Lord (Psalm 23)**

- **Elohim** *(Hebrew: The Lord)* - Exodus 6:3- The first word in Scripture used for God. Elohim expresses the general idea of greatness and glory. It contains the idea of His creative and governing power.

- **Jehovah** *(Hebrew: Lord- YAHWEH)* - Exodus 6:3-God is absolutely self-existent. Revelation 1:8-11, Genesis 1:1

- **God Almighty** *(Hebrew: El Shaddai)* – The word is translated "almighty" and suggest the all-powered nature of God. Shaddai is connected with the Hebrew word that signifies one who nourishes, supplies, and satisfies. The concept of abundance is inextricably intertwined with this great name of God.

The Redemptive Names Are:

JEHOVAH-JIREH
"The Lord our provider" - This is also the name Abraham gave to the place where the Lord provided a sacrifice in exchange for Isaac (Gen. 22:12, 13, 14; Psalms 37:25, Philippians 4:13-19).

JEHOVAH –m' KADDESH:
"God who sanctifies *(Leviticus 20:8)* - "Sanctifies" means to dedicate, to consecrate, to make holy, or to set apart or separate. Holiness is the most impressive of all the attributes of God. It constitutes His fullness and His perfection.

JEHOVAH-NISSI
-"God, our banner- He is a banner of love and protection" – Also, this is the name Moses gave to the altar he built after defeating the Amalekites (Ex. 17:8, 13-16).

JEHOVAH-RAAH
"God, our Shepherd- He tenderly leads us, loves us and will keep us safe." The famous Psalm 23 tells us that, "The Lord

is our Shepherd and we shall not want...." Being illustrated as a shepherd implies a relationship with His sheep (His believers). The term shepherd appears approximately 80 times in the scriptures, detonating characteristics of a feeder, keeper, companion, friend, pastor and herdsman.

JEHOVAH RAMIAH
"Jehovah is exalted" (Ezra 10:10, 11, 25, 44).

JEHOVAH RAAMIAH
This perhaps means "Jehovah has thundered" (Nehemiah 7:7).

JEHOVAH RAPHA
"I am the Lord Your Physician or I am the Lord Your Healer. This name especially was a Name God prophetically spoke about Himself and not one that someone gave Him (Exodus 15:26).

JEHOVAH-ROHI
"Jehovah is my shepherd" (Psalms 23).

JEHOVAH-SABAOTH
"The Lord of Hosts and our Protector"- C.H. Spurgeon said this about the phrase "*The Lord of Hosts*: Isaiah 2:12, 47:4, Matthew 4:11; Luke 2:8-20

The Lord rules the angels, the stars, the elements, and all the hosts of Heaven; and the Heaven of heavens is under His sway... [The Lord] is on our side -- our august Ally; woe unto those who fight against Him, for they shall flee like smoke before the wind when He gives the word to scatter them."

JEHOVAH-SHALOM
"God, our perfect peace"–This is the name Gideon gave to the altar he built at Ophrah (Judges 6:22-24, Isaiah26:3, Psalm 29:11,John 14:27;Philippians 4:7).

JEHOVAH-SHAMMAH
"The One Who is with us everywhere for He is Omnipresent" - The Jerusalem of Ezekiel's vision (see Ezekiel 48:35 margin) was known by this name. Compare text at Isaiah 60:19-20, 2 Chronicles 16:9, Psalm 113:4-6,Psalm 139: 7-8, Proverbs 15:3, Isaiah 43:2 and Acts 17:27-28, Revelation 21:3.

JEHOVAH-TSID-KENU
"The Lord is our righteousness" - The name is applied to a future Davidic king who would lead His people to do what is right and thus bring peace (Psalm 23; 24:5, Psalm 36:6,51:12; Psalm 119:137, Psalms 116:5, Psalm 145:17, Jeremiah 23:6, Romans 3:22) and restoration to the city of Jerusalem (Psalm 71:20, Psalm 40:1-2, Jeremiah 30:17; 33:16, Joel 2:25, Zechariah 9:12, Acts 3:21, Rev 21:4). The name is possibly a play on the name of Zedekiah which means "Righteous [is] the Lord." Zedekiah reigned from 597 to 587 B.C.(See text at Psalm 46:7).

Character traits of God:

God is love. He wants to love, nurture, and help us prosper, if we obey the word *(2 Chronicles 26:5; Ephesians 2:4-5, John 3:16, 1 John 4:7,8,16; Galatians 2:20; John 14:6, 1 Cor. 13, Rom. 5:8).*

God is just. He is "just" in the sense of "fairness." He does not dictate or compel anyone to do anything that he or she does not desire to do.

He merely and sufficiently enlightens, encourages, and presents the opportunity to make a decision to choose right over wrong, but in the same instance, He makes one aware of the repercussions that will occur from those choices *(Isa. 45:21, Zep. 3:5, Luke 18:7, 8; Deut. 32:4; John 5:20; Jos. 24:15, Job 34:12, Isaiah 61:8, Matthew 5:45, Isaiah 55:11, Colossians 3:25).*

God is jealous. *(Exodus 20:3-5, Exodus 34:14, Deuteronomy 4:24, 5:9, 6:15, Psalm 79:5-7, Joshua 24:19-20 Ezekiel 23:25, 2 Cor. 11:2,)* He does not want us to love anyone or anything more than Him.

God is vengeful. He will not always tolerate sin in our lives nor will He allow anyone to inflict hurt towards His children. God will apply or allow chastisement to come upon His children if disobedient to Him or if one offends His children *(Book of Jonah, Jeremiah 31:18, Isaiah 34 chapter, Matt. 18:6-10;*

Rom. 13:18-19; Deuteronomy 32:35, Proverbs 6:34, Psalm 94:1, Hebrews 10:30, Luke 17:2, Romans 12:17-21, Isaiah 35:4).

God is sovereign, orderly, and decent.
God is the spirit who always injects changes for the "enhancement" and prosperity of mankind. He does not work unseemly nor does anything immoral. He is not the author of confusion *(Psalm 37:23; 1 Cor. 14:33; 14:40, James 1).*

When judgment day comes, no man will have an excuse (Rom. 2:1). God allows mankind to choose his or her own destiny based on the choices they make *(Matt. 6:24; Luke 16:24).*

- **God is good.** *(Rom 2:4, Matthew 19:7, James 1:17)*
- **God is wise.** *(Proverbs 2:6; Rom. 11:33)*
- **God is longsuffering.** *(Isaiah 30:18; 2 Peter 3:9, Romans 9:22)*
- **God is merciful and gracious.** *(Matthew 5:7; Psalms 67:1, Psalm 136, Psalm 145, Lamentations 3:22-23, Romans 9:22, Nehemiah 9:31)*

II. *GOD THE SON (Christology)*

- We believe that Jesus Christ is the Son of God and the second person in the Godhead.

- We believe that Jesus was and is eternal in His person and nature as the Son of God who was with God in the beginning of creation.

- We believe that Jesus Christ, the Son of God, was born of a Virgin called Mary according to the scripture St. Matthew 1:18. This therefore gives rise to our fundamental belief in the Virgin Birth and all the miraculous events surrounding this Phenomenon (St. Matthew 1:18). Jesus being this Logos also assumes the title for "Son" and the role of "Son-ship" and has in the scripture referred to his Father as Father or "Father in Heaven".

- We believe that Jesus Christ, the Son of God, served his paternal father, Joseph, in the City of Nazareth, and Judea, and that during his earthly ministry preached the Gospel and performed miracles in the area of the Sea of Galilee.

- We believe that Jesus Christ, the Son of God, became the man, the "Suffering Servant." We believe that Christ while in human form was both 100% man and 100% God. The Suffering Servant came seeking to redeem man from sin and to reconcile him back to God, His Father (Rom. 5:10).

- We believe that Jesus Christ, the Son of God, is standing now as the mediator between God and Man (1 Tim. 2:5). This we believe He shall do until the final overthrow of Satan and evil in the Final Judgment.

- We believe Christ is omnipotent (Matt. 28:18) and omnipresent (Matt. 18:20). He is "The Word" made manifest in the flesh (John 1:1-12). We believe that Jesus possesses the gift "word of knowledge" but he is not all knowing.(Matthew 9:4, Mark 13:32, Matthew 24:36)

The names also attributed to Christ to express his divine nature are:

- The Son of God/Lamb of God: (Matt. 8:29, 14:33, 16:16, 26:33; 27:43; St. John 1:29)

- The First and the Last: (Revelation 1:17)

- The Alpha and Omega: (Rev. 22:13)

- The Word: (John 1:1)

- The Wonderful Counselor: (Isaiah 9:6)

- The Mighty God: (Isaiah 9:6)

- The Everlasting Father: (Isaiah 9:6)

- The Prince of Peace: (Isaiah 9:6)

Jesus Christ is eternal and is "The Word" spoken by God, the father, during the course of creation (John 1:1). Since Christ is incorporated within the bosom, aura or being of

God, He is also the creator of all substance, both physical and spiritual. Christ is the only spiritual entity that has the authority and commission to forgive sins (Luke 7:48). He and the saints of God will be the ones to judge all of mankind and the angels (1 Cor. 6:2,3; John 5:22) Christ is pre-existent and self-existent. He is "The Word" made manifest in the flesh.

III. <u>*GOD, THE SPIRIT (Pneumatology)*</u>

As the C.A.T.B. *(Church According to Bible)* movement, which is part of the Pentecostal movement, we believe that the Holy Ghost is the gift from God that is incorporated within the essence, the bosom, and the aura of His being and was sent to dwell in us as believers. The Spirit was given to empower us to be an anointed witness and render gifts to us to edify the church. He came to be a comforter to the body of Christ. The Holy Ghost is a moving and vitalizing breath which came down at Pentecost as a rushing mighty wind to bring the very presence of God in and around the waiting disciples. As a result, they were filled with the Holy Ghost and began to speak with other tongues, as the Spirit gave them utterance (Acts 4:31; 8:14-17; 10:44-46, 11:15; 19:2-6, Eph. 1:13).

We believe the Holy Ghost or Holy Spirit is the third person of the Godhead, proceeds from the Father and the Son, is of the same substance, equal to power and glory, and is together with the Father and the Son, to be believed in, obeyed, and worshipped. The Holy Ghost is a gift bestowed upon the believer for the purpose of equipping and empowering the believer and making him a more effective witness for service in the world. He teaches and guides one into all truth (John 16:13; Acts 1:8, 8:39).

We believe that the Baptism of the Holy Ghost is an experience subsequent to conversion and sanctification and that tongue-speaking is the consequence of the baptism in the Holy Ghost with the manifestations of the fruit of the spirit (Galatians 5:22-23; Acts 10:46, 19:1-6).

To be filled with the Spirit means to be Spirit controlled as expressed by Paul in Ephesians 5:18-19. Since the charismatic demonstrations were necessary to help the early church to be successful in implementing the command of Christ, we therefore, believe that a Holy Ghost experience is mandatory for all men today and should be sought after with an earnest desire.

We believe that we are not baptized with the Holy Ghost in order to be saved, but that we are baptized with the Holy Ghost because we are saved and will gain more power and effectiveness to be witnesses(Acts 15:8, Acts 29:1-6, John 3:5).

We believe when one receives a baptismal Holy Ghost experience, one will speak a language or tongue according to the sovereign will of Christ that could be unknown to oneself (Acts 2:4).

DOCTRINE OF GOD-HEADTOLOGY

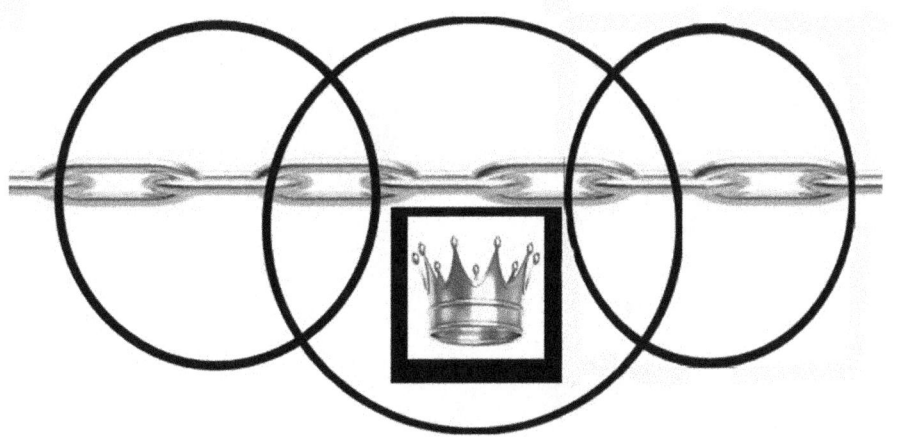

(Our Symbol for God-Headtology)
Chained together as one spirit
(servant-hood to the Father's will)

DOCTRINE OF GOD-HEADTOLOGY

We Believe In:

IV. THE GODHEAD

We believe that the God-Head *(Acts 17:29, Colossians 2:9)* is made up of the Father, the Son, and the Holy Ghost. We believe that each personality of the Godhead are one spirit which is classified as being eternally powerful on heaven and earth and the one who testifies or bear record in heaven *(Romans 1:20, John 10:30, 1 John 5:7)*. Although they are one in spirit, they all have different functions and God the Father is the supreme authority of the Godhead. This is proven by what Christ stated in the following scriptures:

John 3:16- For God so loved the world, that he gave his only begotten Son, that whosoever believeth in him should not perish, but have everlasting life.

John 6:38-For I came down from heaven, not to do mine own will, but the will of him that sent me.

Romans 8:34-Who *is* he that condemneth? *It is* Christ that died, yea rather, that is risen again, who is even at the right hand of God, who also maketh intercession for us.

God the Father is in charge. He is the one who controls things. The scriptures clearly show us through the words of Jesus Christ that only God knows when the gathering "rapture" is going to take place. Jesus states in Matthew 24:36-But concerning that day and hour no one knows, not even the angels of heaven, nor the Son, but the Father only.

All three are worthy and honorable of due benevolence, the upmost respect, and praise.

> The word "Godhead" occurs in the King James Version only 3 times - Acts 17:29; Rom 1:20; Col. 2:9, and it translate slightly different each time though closely related (In Greek-*theion, theiotes, theotes*). Theion means "that which is divine." Paul uses this word in Acts 17:29 in an address made to a heathen audience. The Greeks used it in the sense of "the Divine Being" and as a general term to designate "the Deity" apart from reference to a particular god. "Godhead" is from two Greek words *theos* and *deitas* combined in Greek?. *theioteôs*. The scriptural term Godhead (KJV) is rendered "divine nature" or "deity"; it means the very *essence* of God. The meaning of the term *"fullness of the godhead"* is that Jesus was fully God on earth just as His Father is fully God in heaven *(John 3:16/John 10:29-31)* and the Holy Ghost is fully God that not only lives

and dwells in us but empowers us to be witnesses and do miracles *(Acts 1:8)*. The point made in this scripture is that Jesus was 100% God and 100% human while living on earth.

Trinity defines <u>God</u> as three divine persons or <u>*hypostases*</u>. We do not declare ourselves as "Trinitarians" because the word "Trinitarian" implies that the three persons of the God-Head are co-equal, co-eternal and <u>consubstantial</u> *(of the same substance and essence)*. We believe the Father, the Son, and the Holy Ghost are:
- Co-equal in "power" only <u>because God the father allows them to be. Jesus is his son, and the Holy Ghost is His gift.</u>
- Co-equal in their effectiveness to get their objective done in the winning of souls and the function of everything created.
- Co-equal in spirit because they are all perfect without sin.
- Consubstantial- of the same substance or essence.

However, they are <u>not</u> co-equal in "authority". It is the authority position that controls the degree of power and knowledge each entity receives. Because God has allowed them to be as one, He has sanctioned them to partake of the same power He has. However, in regards to knowledge, Jesus and the Holy Ghost are not "all knowing" because Matthew 24:36 proves that only God the father knows when the gathering or rapture will take place and He will give the orders because He is in charge of the process. Christ made it clear to us when He stated in John 6:38- **"For I came down from heaven, not to do mine own will, but the will of him that sent me."**

They work together in order to flow as an unbeatable force that affects the heavens, the earth, hell and the universe around them. They flow together in the order that God the Father prescribed to perpetuate His will. *(Matthew 28:18, 1 Corinthians 14:40)* And because the order of the Godhead operates and flows according to God the Father's Authority, we classify ourselves as "God-Headtologist". This is a word created by our organization which means one who believes in the power, the function, and the order of which God the father ordains through the persons (Jesus and Holy Spirit) of the God-Head to carry out His Will. We believe that they are one in the spirit in that they are sub- servant to God's will without doubt, question or resistance. We believe that all three persons in the Godhead contribute to the creation according to God's command.

That is certified by Genesis 1:26-28 and John 1:1-3:

Genesis 1:26-28

And God said, Let us make man in our image, after our likeness: and let them have dominion over the fish of the sea, and over the fowl of the air, and over the cattle, and over all the earth, and over every creeping thing that creepeth upon the earth.

²⁷ So God created man in his own image, in the image of God created he him; male and female created he them.

²⁸ And God blessed them, and God said unto them, Be fruitful, and multiply, and replenish the earth, and subdue it: and have dominion over the fish of the sea, and over the fowl of the air, and over every living thing that moveth upon the earth.

John 1:1-3
New King James Version (NKJV)
The Eternal Word
1 In the beginning was the Word, and the Word was with God, and the Word was God. ² He was in the beginning with God. ³ All things were made through Him, and without Him nothing was made that was made.

TO GOD BE THE GLORY!

DOCTRINE OF MAN

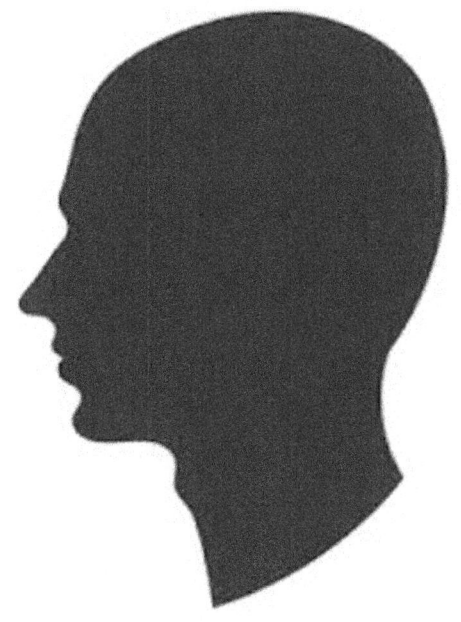

The Components that Build and
Hurt Man Spiritually

DOCTRINE OF MAN

We Believe in:

THE DOCTRINE OF MAN:
We believe that man was created holy by God and is composed of body and soul. We believe that man by nature is born sinful and unholy because of the Adamic sin that occurred in the Garden of Eden(Genesis 3:6). Being born in sin, he needs to be born again, sanctified and cleansed by the blood of Jesus. We believe that man is saved by confessing and forsaking his sins and believing on the Lord Jesus Christ. We believe that after being born again and adopted into the family of God, man may and should claim the inheritance of the sons of God, namely, the baptism of the Holy Ghost (Psalm 8:4-9; Romans 10:9-10).

SALVATION
Salvation deals with the application of the work of redemption to the sinner with his restoration to divine favor and communion with God. This redemptive operation of the Holy Ghost upon sinners is brought about by repentance towards God and faith towards our Lord Jesus Christ. This in turn results in conversion, justification, regeneration, sanctification, and the baptism of the Holy Ghost.

Repentance is the work of God, which results in a change of mind in respect to man's relationship to God (St. Matthew 3:1-2, 4:17; Acts 20:21).

Faith is a certain conviction wrought in the heart by the Holy Spirit, as to the truth of the Gospel and a heart trust in the promises of God (Romans 1:17, 3:28; St. Matthew 9:22; Acts 26:18).

Conversion is that act of God whereby He causes the regenerated sinner, in his conscious life, to turn to Him in repentance and faith (II Kings 5:15; II Chronicles 33:12-13; St. Luke 19:8, 9; Acts 8:30).

Regeneration is that act of God by which the principle of the new life is implanted in man, and the governing disposition of the soul is made holy and secured.

Sanctification is that gracious and continuous operation of the Holy Ghost by which He delivers the justified sinner from the pollution of sin, renews his whole nature in the image of God, and enables him to perform good works (Romans 6:4; 5:6; Colossians 2:12; 3:1).

ANGELS

The Bible uses the term "angel", a heavenly body, clearly and primarily to denote messengers or ambassadors of God with such scripture references as Revelations 4:5 which indicates that their duty in heaven is to praise God, Psalm 103:20, to do God's will, and St. Matthew 18:10, to behold his face. But since angels must come down to earth, they also have a mission to earth. The Bible indicates that angels accompanied God in the Creation and will also accompany Christ in His return in Glory.

THE BIBLE

We believe that the Bible is the word of God and contains one harmonious and sufficiently complete system of doctrine. We believe in the full inspiration of the word of God. We hold the word of God to be the only authority in all matters and assert that no doctrine can be true or essential if it does not find a place in this word. We believe as stated in II Timothy 3:16,"All scripture *is* given by inspiration of God, and *is* profitable for doctrine, for reproof, for correction, for instruction in righteousness:" (2 Timothy 2:15). Reading the word of God faithfully builds up one's ability to discern right from wrong situations and stay in the knowledge of the truth (Psalm 119:105; Psalm 119:11). We believe the bible is the only book in the world that contains the infallible truth given by the inspiration of God in its entirety.

STATISTICS FOR THE BIBLE

The Bible can be read aloud in **70 hours**.

There are **8,674 different Hebrew words** in the Bible, **5,624 different Greek words**, and **12,143 different English words** in the King James Version.

Number of books in the Bible: 66 Chapters: 1,189 Verses: 31,102 Words: 783,137 Letters: 3,116,480 Number of promises that are given in the Bible: 1,260 Commands: 6,468 Predictions: over 8,000 Fulfilled prophecy: 3,268 verses Unfulfilled prophecy: 3,140 Number of questions: 3,294 Longest name: Mahershalalhashbaz (Isaiah 8:1) Longest verse: Esther 8:9 (78 words) Shortest verse: John 11:35 (2 words: "Jesus wept"). This is the King James Bible. Some Bibles might be Job 3:2 (Job said.), but King James has that as "Job answered" which is longer than Jesus wept. Middle books: Micah and Nahum Middle verse: Psalm 103:2-3 Middle chapter: Psalm 117 Shortest chapter (by number of words): Psalm 117 (by number of words) Longest book: Psalms (150 chapters) Shortest book (by number of words): 3 John Longest chapter: Psalm 119 (176 verses) Number of times the word "God" appears: 4,094 Number of times the word "Lord" appears: 6,781 Number of different authors: 40 Number of languages the Bible has been translated into: over 1,200 OLD TESTAMENT STATISTICS (King James Authorized): Number of books: 39 Chapters: 929 Verses: 23,145 Words: 602,585 Letters: 2,278,100 Middle book: Proverbs Middle chapter: Job 20 Middle verses: 2 Chronicles 20:17,18 Smallest book: Obadiah Shortest Verse: 1 Chronicles 1:25 Longest verse: Esther 8:9 Longest chapter: Psalms 119 Largest book: Psalms NEW TESTAMENT STATISTICS: Number of books: 27 Chapters: 260 Verses: 7,957 Words: 180,552 Letters: 838,380 Middle book: 2 Thessalonians Middle chapters: Romans 8, 9 Middle verse: Acts 27:17 Smallest book: 3 John Shortest verse: John 11:35 Longest verse: Revelation 20:4 Longest chapter: Luke 1 Largest book:

PRAYER

We believe that prayer is essential for living a steadfast and righteous life. Prayer is the practice that keeps a person flexible, susceptible, keen, passionate, and adherent to the will and move of God. We believe that it is impossible to be a strong, mature, woman or man of God without prayer being inclusive in one's life. We base this belief on the following scriptures:

Luke 18:1- And he spake a parable unto them to this end, that men ought always to pray, and not to faint;

1 Thessalonians 5:16-17- Rejoice evermore. Pray without ceasing.

Ephesians 6:18- Praying always with all prayer and supplication in the Spirit, and watching thereunto with all perseverance and supplication for all saints;

FASTING

We believe that fasting is an essential needed in gaining a powerful anointing in Christ. We believe there are various fast that accomplish different things in a person's life. We believe that whichever fast is chosen, if rendered to the glory of God it will yield both spiritual and physical discipline. In addition, one will gain a greater anointing and insight in their walk with God."

(**Special Note:** *We recommend to everyone who takes medication to please consult with their doctor before attempting any of the fast listed below.)*

The following are the types of fast endorsed by the C.A.T.B.:

A straight or water fast.- We believe this fast is the most effective for breaking stronghold's such as bad habits, illnesses, sinful behavioral traits *(i.e.-homosexuality, fornication, adultery, porno addiction, alcoholism, drug addiction, meanness, jealousy, spoiledness, anger, gluttony, greed, etc.)* In other words, this type of fast can destroy the lust of the flesh, the lust of the eye, and the pride of life. We believe this fast brings on a greater anointing to heal the sick and lame, perform miracles, dispel demons, sharpen prophecies, and achieve a higher level of wisdom all in and under the name of Christ Jesus.

   A straight or water fast spiritually prepares one to receive the baptism of the Holy Ghost! Christ made it clear in Mark 9:29 when he stated, "And he said unto them, **This kind** *(strongholds)***can come forth by nothing, but by prayer and fasting**." In 1 Corinthians 9:27 Paul stated, "But I keep under my body, and bring [it] into subjection: lest that by any means, when I have preached to others, I myself should be a castaway. " A straight fast <u>builds self-control!</u> In addition, it is most effective when faith, bible reading, constant prayer, love, obedience and a consecrated conversation are rendered with it. Just going without food is not enough. Without these added essentials, fasting would be only **<u>a diet.</u>**

   Daniel fast- This fast is great for obtaining spiritual and physical discipline. This fast is designed for eating only fruits and vegetables or vegetarian based products *(no egg beaters)*. It excludes all dairy, poultry and meat products. However, 100% fruit juices and fruit smoothies *(without dairy products)* are accepted.

   <u>**Sacrificial fast-**</u> This fast deals with giving up things that are classified as weaknesses, hindrances or distractions in one's

life for an ordained period of time. Things that can distort spiritual and physical progression such as: television, sweets, video games, social media, breads, sodas and high caffeine based energy drinks like coffee, etc., etc. We based this fast on the following scripture: Hebrews 12:1-" Wherefore seeing we also are compassed about with so great a cloud of witnesses, let us lay aside every weight, and the sin which doth so easily beset us, and let us run with patience the race that is set before us…"

1 Corinthians 11:28-31-

<u>But let a man examine himself</u>, and so let him eat of that bread, and drink of that cup.

For he that eateth and drinketh unworthily, eateth and drinketh damnation to himself, not discerning the Lord's body.

For this cause many are weak and sickly among you, and many sleep.

<u>For if we would judge ourselves</u>, we should not be judged.

Once again, all types of fast must be done with faith, bible reading, constant prayer, love, obedience and a consecrated conversation.

We believe these fast bring closeness, higher reverence, a deeper love, and an increased anointing from God if done with a sincere heart. This is certified by Matthew 5:6, **"Blessed are they who do hunger and thirst after righteousness: for they shall be filled."**

THE CHURCH

The Church forms a spiritual unity of which Christ is the divine head. It is animated by one Spirit; the Spirit of Christ. It professes one faith, shares one hope, and serves one King. It is the citadel of the truth and God's agency for communicating to believers all spiritual blessings. The Church then is the object of our faith rather than of knowledge.

The name of our Church, **"C.A.T.B."(Church According to Bible),** is supported by 2 Timothy 3:16 and other passages in the Pauline Epistles. The word **"CHURCH"** or **"EKKLESIA"** was first applied to the Christian society by Jesus Christ in St. Matthew 16:18 with the occasion being that of his benediction of Peter at Caesarea Philippi. We believe no matter how things change in the world, the bible *(from the King James Version(KJV)*, if carried out in its' context and procedure as given by the men of God who wrote under the anointing of God, yet holds the truth on how we as the church must operate doctrinally and handle all matters of concern. We believe the King James Version of 1611 (KJV) is the supreme interpretation of the bible despite the number of translators who contributed to this edition. We stand on this premise by faith and the belief "that God is just" according to Deut. 32:4 which states," He is the Rock, his work is perfect: for all his ways are judgment: a God of truth and without iniquity, just and right is He." Because God is not the author of confusion *(1 Corinthians 14:33)*, He would not leave us ignorant when it comes to living for Him and getting closer to Him. God is the one who controls and orchestrates all things that give glory to His name. James 1:17 states," Every good gift and every perfect gift is from above, and cometh down from the Father of lights, with whom is no variableness, neither shadow of turning." We believe that the longevity of this translation to stand (403 years) is the manifestation that the anointing of God rest on this bible. We believe that the results achieved such as healing, deliverance, and miracles while one lives out the commandments written in the word is the manifestation of God's anointing in real time (Isaiah 55:11).

We believe that the validity of other translations of the bible must measure up to and maintain the context of the King James Version that has already been presented and established in the scriptures over the test of time.

THE SECOND COMING OF CHRIST

We believe in the second coming of Christ; that He shall come from heaven to earth, personally, bodily, visibly (Acts 1:11; Titus 2:11-13; St. Matthew 16:27; 24:30; 25:30; Luke 21:27; John 1:14, 17; Titus 2:11) and that the Church, the bride, will be caught up to meet Him in the air (I Thessalonians, 4:16-17). We admonish all who have this hope to purify themselves as He is pure.

DIVINE HEALING

The **Church According To Bible** believes in and practices divine healing. It is a commandment of Jesus to the Apostles (St. Mark 16:18). Jesus affirms his teachings on healing by explaining to His disciples, who were to be Apostles, that healing the afflicted is by faith (St. Luke 9:40-41). Therefore, we believe that healing by faith in God has scriptural support and ordained authority. St. James' writing in his epistle encourages Elders to pray for the sick, lay hands upon them, and to anoint them with oil, and that prayers with faith shall heal the sick and the Lord shall raise them up. Healing is still practiced in C.A.T.B., and testimonies of healing in our Church testify to this fact. (1 Peter 2:24; James 5:14-16)

MIRACLES

The **Church According To Bible** believes that miracles occur to convince men that the Bible is God's Word. A miracle can be defined as an extraordinary visible act of divine power, wrought by the efficient agency of the will of God, which has as its final cause the vindication of the righteousness of God's word. We believe that the works of God, which were performed during the beginnings of Christianity, do and will occur even today where God is preached, Faith in Christ is exercised, the Holy Ghost is active, and the gospel is promulgated in the truth. (Acts 5:15; 6:8; 9:40; Luke 4:36, 7:14-15; 5:5-6; St. Mark 14:15).

THE ORDINANCES OF THE CHURCH

It is generally admitted that for an ordinance to be valid, it must have been instituted by Christ. When we speak of ordinances of the church, we are speaking of those instituted by Christ, in which by sensible signs the grace of God in Christ, and the benefits of the covenant of grace are represented, sealed, and applied to believers, and these in turn give expression to their faith and allegiance to God. The *Church According To Bible* recognizes three ordinances as having been instituted by Christ himself and are therefore binding upon the church practice.

A. THE LORD'S SUPPER (HOLY COMMUNION)

The Lord's Supper symbolizes the Lord's death and suffering in place of His people. It also symbolizes the believer's participation in the crucified Christ. It represents not only the death of Christ as the object of faith which unites the believers to Christ, but also the effect of this act as the giving of life, strength, and joy to the soul. The communicant by faith enters into a special spiritual union of his soul with the glorified Christ. (1 Corinthians 11:23-33)

B. FEET WASHING

Feet Washing is practiced and recognized as an ordinance in our church because Christ, by His example, showed that humility characterized greatness in the Kingdom of God, and that service, rendered to others gave evidence that humility, motivated by love, exists. These services are held subsequent to the Lord's Supper; however, its regularity is left to the discretion of the pastor in charge. (John 13:1-17) We also believe that the foot washing done by Christ is a revelation that spiritually symbolizes that a believer's steps are ordered and empowered by Christ (Psalms 37:23) when washed in the power of the Holy Ghost. The Holy Ghost intensifies our steps and our witness. (Holy Ghost symbolized as living water- John 7:38; John 13:8)

C. WATER BAPTISM

We believe that Water Baptism is necessary as instructed by Christ in St. John 3:5 which states, **"UNLESS MAN BE BORN AGAIN OF WATER AND OF THE SPIRIT."**

However, we do <u>not</u> believe that water baptism alone is a means of salvation (Luke 23:38-43), but is an outward demonstration that one has already had a conversion experience and has accepted Christ as his personal Savior. Immersion corresponds more closely to death, burial, and resurrection of our Lord (Colossians 2:12).

Water Baptism also symbolizes the regeneration and purification of man. Therefore, we practice total immersion as our mode of baptism. We believe that we should use the Baptismal Formula given to us by Christ for all **"…IN THE NAME OF THE FATHER, AND OF THE SON, AND OF THE HOLY GHOST."** (St. Matthew 28:19)

We believe that the **"SPRINKLING"** of water is a way of dedicating a child to God (The appropriate age is 1-5 years for *christening and circumcision*).On the other hand, the total submersion in water is for a person who has an understanding of what baptism is all about, consciously received Jesus Christ as their Lord and Savior, and died to sin. *(The appropriate age is approximately 6 years and up)* We base this belief on the scriptures: (Hebrews 10:22, Luke 2:21-38, Ezekiel 36:25, Matt. 3:13-17)

D. TITHES AND OFFERING

We believed in the giving of tithes *(10% of your gross earnings specified as first-fruits)* and offering for the support of the pastor, the church, and the betterment of the people of God and the work of God <u>faithfully</u>. We based this belief on the scriptures Malachi 3:6-10 and Acts 2:43-46. We believe that the tithing is an act of giving influenced by the love and appreciation to God which was first inspired by Abraham and Jacob. (Genesis 14:17-24; Genesis 28:20-22, and Hebrews 7:1-28)

Since we are the spiritual seed of Abraham (Galatians 3:29), we are held to the covenant that was made by our forefathers.

This shows that tithing was before the law, during the law, after the law, and is now and forever. For even Jesus stated in Matt. 23:23,"Woe unto you, scribes and Pharisees, hypocrites! for ye pay tithe of mint and anise and cummin, and have omitted the weightier [matters] of the law, judgment, mercy, and faith: <u>these ought ye to have done, and not to leave the other undone.</u>"This is also proven in <u>Luke 11:42 which states,</u>" But woe unto you, Pharisees! For ye tithe mint and rue and all manner of herbs, and pass over judgment and the love of God: <u>these ought ye to have done, and not to leave the other undone.</u>"

Tithing should be given with love, faith, and trust in God. Other supporting scriptures include Proverbs 3:9, Mark 12:17, Luke 6:38, 2 Corinthians 9:6-8, and 1 Timothy 5:17.

SIN

The Bible teaches that sin began in the angelic world (Ezekiel 28:11-19 and Isaiah 14:12-20), and is transmitted into the blood of the human race through disobedience and deception motivated by unbelief (I Timothy 2:14). Adam's sin, committed by eating of the forbidden fruit from the tree of knowledge of good and evil, carried with it permanent pollution or depraved human nature to all his descendants. This is called **"original sin."** Sin can now be defined as a volitional transgression against God and a lack of conformity to the will of God. We, therefore, conclude that man by nature, is sinful and that he has fallen from a glorious and righteous state from which he was created, and has become unrighteous and unholy. Man, therefore, must be restored to his state of holiness from which he has fallen by being born again (St. John 3:7).

Many of the doctrinal writings of our belief were transcribed from the COGIC Handbook because many of our beliefs are the same; however, there are some slight belief changes and elaborations that have been incorporated into the C.A.T.B. handbook which sets us apart. It is not denomination that gets you to heaven but its Holy Living and belief in Our Lord and Savior, Jesus Christ.

TO GOD BE THE GLORY!

DOCTRINE OF ROLE SHIP

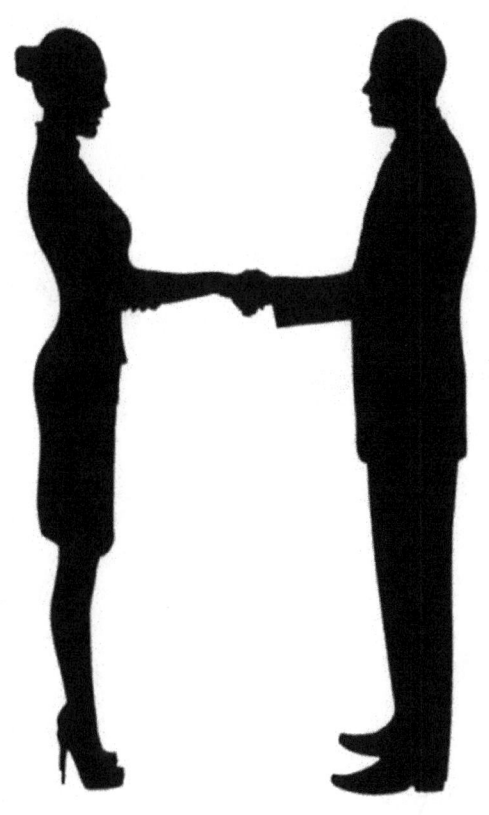

DOCTRINE OF ROLE SHIP

We believe that the **"Doctrine of Role Ship"** is vitally important in the development of men and women to the fullest. We believe it is in the understanding and implementation of our "gender" roles according to the word of God which helps fortify the innate behavioral traits that God has instilled in each gender from the start. The carrying out of the roles is what acts as a living subliminal message that reminds us of the positioning which God intended for each gender to hold. Pride, sin, "male abandonment", drugs and "single parenting" are causes that has contributed to the role "break down" globally. In other words, it's primarily the man's fault that caused the total emerging of sin to come into this world and initiated the human race to lose the "perfect state" that God made them! (Genesis 3:5-7)

MAN:

We believe that "man" was created to be the head caretaker of this world, the leading component in the structure of the church, and the leading entity of a marital relationship. We believe that the man is the protector of the wife and the headship of the family. Man was designed for "War" in handling the toughest interaction of a battle be it spiritual or natural. (Exodus 17:9)

It is for this purpose that Jesus chose twelve "men" to be the ones to start and build the church foundation (Matthew 10:2-4) and one of them was a betrayer. Even when they replaced Judas Iscariot, they replaced him with another man, Matthias (Acts 1: 12-26) He did not choose twelve men simply for cultural reasons, but it was for carrying out God's divine will. (John 6:38)

In order to be a mature man of Christ in a marriage, one must love his wife, and submit to his wife as she submits to him (Eph. 5, 21). We base this premises on the following scriptures: Genesis 1-2; 1 Corinthians 11:1-16, Ephesians 5:23, 1Timothy 2:12 (situational), Titus 2:1-5, Ephesians 5:25.

Likewise, ye husbands, dwell with *them* according to knowledge, giving honour unto the wife, as unto the weaker vessel, and as being heirs together of the grace of life; that your prayers be not hindered. We believe and teach that the man is not the "boss" of the wife, but the "leader and director" that organizes his own family according to their personal strengths which in turn will yield an effective and progressive spiritual unit. (1 Timothy 3:5)

We believe that the man is the glory of God and the woman is the glory of man as it is states in 1 Corinthians 11:7- For a man indeed ought not to cover *his* head, forasmuch as he is the image and glory of God: but the woman is the glory of the man.

This means that because man was first created in his image and likeness he reflects God and the woman, in her general nature in this earthly and temporal dispensation, reflects the glory of man. Matthew Henry puts it like this man is the sun and the woman is the moon that is the reflection of the sun. We believe that every holy man should strive to possess the characteristics that the word of God has prescribed us to seek for. These characteristics and behavioral traits are as follows:

- He is firm footed, not fickle
- He holds his tongue. He thinks before he speaks.
- He gives good biblical advice.
- He is admired by his peers
- He strives to obtain wisdom continually
- He stays calm when insulted
- He accepts rebukes from his father
- He thinks ahead
- He surrounds himself and communes with other holy men.
- His conversation is sound and respected by others
- He is cautious and avoids danger
- He is patience and calm. Not short-tempered
- He regards his father's advice
- He hungers for the truth
- He is a peacemaker
- He is one who trust in the Lord and seeks direction

- He allows God to direct him in finding a wife
- He believes and is given over to a routine life of prayer, fasting and reading the word of God
- If married, he provides for his family and he loves his wife like Christ loves the church
- He is concerned about God's people
- He is obedient and respectful to his pastor
- He leads his family to church and stays there. *(Does not drop them off)*
- He is a cheerful and liberal giver *(ie-a tither)*
- He is concerned about the well-being of fatherless boys who don't have a role model.
- He is industrious
- He is not selfish
- He does not beat or abuse women in any way
- He is not boisterous, but humble
  (Scriptures that support these standpoints will be taught in the doctrinal classes)

WOMAN:

We believe that the woman was created to be the "help mete" to man and as vessels of ministry to glorify God. (Genesis 2:18; Acts 2:17) states- And the LORD God said, It is not good that the man should be alone; I will make him a helper suitable for him. Women were created to be a nurturer, a companion, a savior, who will help generate life and usher the man towards that light of Christ and the achievement of purpose.

They are the spiritual friend aligned up to be as one with their mate to help sharpened and be sharpen like iron sharpens iron. (Proverbs 27:17) Women are identified as the "weaker" vessel in 1 Peter 3:7 in physical strength, but not in intellect or ingenuity. Just asked Deborah who God chose to be a judge during a time when men were deficient in spiritual fortitude and faith. Even scriptures regarded Deborah as a <u>mother in Israel</u> who arose. (Judges 5:7) Even she strived to render the final victory to a man, Barak. No matter who you talk to or how they exegesis the scriptures they will never find a woman who occupied a pastoral position in the bible.

Many male pastors state we need not worry about that and stop spending time on that subject. It's fatuous and a waste of time. **Point of interest:** Everything that God says and does not say is pertinent. The doctrine of role ship is designed for gender conditioning by His standards not ours. God never does anything haphazardly. He lets us know do not add to his word. (Proverbs 30:5-6) We do believe that women can be placed in a position of an overseer or nurturer to temporarily hold a people together until a "man" of God is raised up to continue the work. As long as they understand and embrace the fact of who they are-"the mother of the house" and what they are called to do. The problem with this is women who serve in this capacity must be wise enough to understand the positioning God has set forth according to his word and for their gender. The word of the Lord is a lamp unto my feet and a light to our pathway. (Psalm 119:105) It is important to keep a "male" covering *(bishop)* over them during this period of time.

Women who serve in this position of female pastoring have a tendency to develop a "feministic, bossy, masculine" behavior. They get addicted to that authority and get blinded when being on the look-out for good male leadership *(prospects)* among the congregation. Show me a female pastor and I will show you a woman who 98% of the time is resistant to male leadership or exemplify a history of poor male interaction due to molestation, abandonment or abuse. If married they are generally bossy and controlling towards their husbands and lack submissiveness.

They exert strong forceful personalities that desire to stay in a controlling position rather than trust in the leadership of a <u>godly</u> man. They easily get disrespectful to the male influence and are argumentative unless the male counterpart is docile in nature. Not trying to be rude or disrespectful, but these are things I have experienced through interaction and research for many years. As people supporting the kingdom we respect these women because we believe in following peace with all men (Hebrews 12:14), but the positioning in which there proclaiming the gospel we are apprehensive and careful because of no scriptural support and the results which they gingerly yield in male development. With the war with alternative lifestyle this subject is a major concern more than ever.

Compare them to a Proverbs 31 woman and they will come up short most of the time. Notice I said "godly". Don't believe me just check it out. For a woman to be strong is alright as long as that strength is governed or geared towards building, encouraging, nurturing the husband and the children, and assisting in raising the family along with their husband or male covering to the glory of God! Strong women should use their wisdom to help build up strong male leadership geared towards building up the families, assisting good pastoral leadership and fulfilling of their purpose. We believe if a woman is a single mother who is rearing up boys, it is imperative for a mother to prayerfully search out trusting men of the church to help with the supervision of those children. The men of the church should be more caring of helping with the male children with proper supervision.

<u>Women are to be honored, respected and loved, NOT BEAT OR INSULTED. (Ephesians 5:28)</u>Key point gentlemen. That is our job and our endeavor as men of God. We believe in rendering respect and due benevolence to the woman in the service of God according to how the word has prescribed. Loving a wife as God loves the church keeps a woman feeling protected, respected and secured. We believe a woman can serve in every office of ministry such as prophecy, evangelism, missionary-ship, and even preach *(proclaim-declare-state the gospel)*, but not pastor. However, in the facet of teaching, there are certain limitations. Women can teach children and other women, but not men. *(18 and up, 1 Timothy 2:12)* Women must stay in the guidelines of Titus 2:4-5 in their preaching.

We believe that every holy woman should strive to possess the characteristics that the word of God has prescribed us to seek for. These characteristics and behavioral traits are as follows:

- She is a committed, loving and caring wife and mother
- She lives for the betterment of her home and family
- She is diligently active, assiduous in work or in study
- She is skillful and clever
- She is self-disciplined and organized
- She is intelligent and a fervent businesswoman
- She is hospitable and graceful
- She is very loving and compassionate in time of need
- She is virtuous because she is spiritually-minded
- She only allows herself to date a man who loves the Lord, and who is sincere in heart and respectful of her gender.
- She is respectful of other holy men and understands the authority ordained to them by God
  (Scriptures that support these standpoints will be taught in the doctrinal classes)

THE DOCTRINE OF PRESENTATION AND SOCIALIZATION

THE DOCTRINE OF PRESENTATION AND SOCIALIZATION

Leviticus 10:10 states-"And that ye may put difference between holy and unholy, and between unclean and clean." **(KJV)**

You are to distinguish between the holy and the common, and between the unclean and the clean. **(ESV)**

Matthew 5:14 - Ye are the light of the world. A city that is set on an hill cannot be hid. **(KJV)**

"You are the light of the world. A city set on a hill cannot be hidden. **(ESV)**

2 Corinthians 3:2-3 - Ye are our epistle written in our hearts, known and read of all men.

Forasmuch as ye are manifestly declared to be the epistle of Christ ministered by us, written not with ink, but with the Spirit of the living God; not in tables of stone, but in fleshy tables of the heart. **(KJV)**

You yourselves are our letter of recommendation, written on our hearts, to be known and read by all. And you show that you are a letter from Christ delivered by us, written not with ink but with the Spirit of the living God, not on tablets of stone but on tablets of human hearts. **(ESV)**

Matthew 7:20 King James Version (KJV)
20 Wherefore by their fruits ye shall know them. (KJV)

1 Peter 2:9- But ye *are* a chosen generation, a royal priesthood, an holy nation, a peculiar people; that ye should shew forth the praises of him who hath called you out of darkness into his marvelous light. **(KJV)**

But you are a chosen race, a royal priesthood, a holy nation, a people for his own possession, that you may proclaim the excellencies of him who called you out of darkness into his marvelous light. **(ESV)**

1 Peter 1:14-16- As obedient children, not fashioning yourselves according to the former lusts in your ignorance: But as he which hath called you is holy, so be ye holy in <u>all manner of conversation</u>; Because it is written, Be ye holy; for I am holy. **(KJV)**

As obedient children, do not be conformed to the passions of your former ignorance, but as he who called you is holy, you also be holy in all your conduct, since it is written, "You shall be holy, for I am holy." **(ESV)**

It is from the following verses that the premise for the "Doctrine of Presentation" and "The Doctrine of Socialization" was developed.

The Doctrine of Presentation and Socialization

"Presentation" is defined as appearance and exhibition. "Socialization" is defined as the process by which children and adults learn from others. We begin learning from others during the early days of life; and most people continue their social learning all through life (unless some mental or physical disability slows or stops the learning process).

The primary verse that brings all these verses together for the C.A.T.B. (Church According To Bible) is 1 Peter 1:14-16. In this verse, Peter makes it clear that we must strive to be holy in all manner of conversation. In every area of communication, holiness must be the key factor that is adhered to. We, *the church*, must be the influential factor for the world and not the world for us.

Communication can be transmitted through sight, touch, smell, voice, hearing and total behavior. God shows us through the witness of the scriptures that we are the ones responsible for making a difference between clean and unclean, and holy and unholy (Lev. 10:10). Everything that we do, create, and interact with, must ultimately be geared towards glorifying God and positioning ourselves to be that light! Even the blind knew and were inspired by Jesus while He was passing through because of the power, love, and life He exemplified

(John 9). We believe that we are the ones that must establish the parameters under the leading of God. Christians must keep the *"lines of difference"* drawn according to the scripture, between saints *(the royal priesthood and chosen generation)* and sinners. We must be careful and cognizant that the lines drawn are according to the teachings of Christ in every area of interaction.

With the rise and legalization of homosexualism, unisexism, and the easy accessibility to lustful entertainment through computer technology and social media, a difference in jewelry and clothing style must be maintained unlike never before. As previously mentioned, Matthew 24:12 states –"And because iniquity shall abound, the love of many shall wax cold". This tells us that sin is filtering into every component of human existence. Sin is being represented and adhered to in the styles of the clothing, entertainment, fine arts, tattoos (and markings), liberal arts, in the church, and in life itself. The media as a whole is being used to desensitize us to sin that God deems abominable.

Even in children movies you will see more subliminal messages that are rendered today to acclimate them to same-sex acceptance. In the movie:"Kindergarten Cop 2" rated PG, they had a beautiful African American (black) girl at the age of 5 say she had two mothers who taught her to not trust men at all.

This is not because God is not powerful enough to keep sin at bay, but many "Christians" welcome the way of the world as a means to be accepted, liked, and enjoy the indulgence of the flesh. Remember, Jehovah gives us freewill. Some Christians are pushed against "the wall of compromise" and others are tired and have gladly surrendered and collapsed to these unwarranted vanities of life. And if you stand for the standards of God you are immediately viewed as **"JUDGMENTAL";** of which many people, even believers, use out of context.

Over fifteen years ago, I prophesied through the release of my book, "COGIC Unsanctioned Issues: Biblical or Trivia?", that the plan of Satan was to formulate a "merged" society. Several believers did not believe or pay attention to this prophecy because at the time I did not have an established ministry.

Some of the disrespect I received was caused by some past unpleasant experiences, and as a result, I was viewed as a little ole preacher just throwing out prophecies for the fun of it. I was judged as a man who was over the top or too traditional.

I declared that we would become a society where the *"identifying characteristics"* of a man and the *"identifying characteristics"* of a woman would be merged together. This in turn would create a generation of people who would develop a "merge belief system". This belief system would slowly deplete the moral fiber of every nation and cause an enormous explosion of confusion, freedom to sin, self-justification, wickedness, and uncontrolled wrath, itching ears and finally genocide of an identified gender.

This in turn would yield a generation of people who would be socialized into three categories: Anti-Christ children with no respect for God, Churches who would have a "form of Godliness and no power", a nomadic generation or "it" society in which "male" and "female" differences would be merged into one mindset or one gender. The "it" society is one that adopts the principle "do as thou wilt" which pushes the doctrine you can be save and do whatever makes you happy, God won't mind.

If God does not come soon, this world will undergo a "hypocrisy brainwash" and be unable to identify the difference between male and female responsibilities in regards to parenting and family development. As it was in the days of Noah so shall it be again (Matt. 24:37). This is all happening today as time is repeating itself. Kids are growing up with male-male (husband and husband) and female-female (wife-wife) parenting. "Same-sex marriages" and "same sex parents" are being advertised as wholesome relationships, wholesome families, and role models while the doctrine of Christ is being ignored.

2 John 1:9 states:

"Whosoever transgresseth, and abideth not in the doctrine of Christ, hath not God. He that abideth in the doctrine of Christ, he hath both the Father and the Son".

Because of all the things going on in the world today, C.A.T.B. believes it is vitally important to project a distinct difference in gender identity so that our children will be able to identify discrete mannerisms pertaining to a developing man and woman of God. For Proverbs 22:6 states: "Train

The Doctrine of Presentation and Socialization

up a child in the way he should go: and when he is old, he will not depart from it." This is done through the "Doctrine of Presentation" and "Doctrine of Socialization".

We believe it is our responsibility to raise our boys to be "masculine" as according to the word of God and our girls to be "feminine" as according to the word of God.

We strive to raise-up Disciples and Proverbs women through godly training and social interaction according to scripture. "Doctrine of Presentation" contributes to that effort. It deals with the outside presentation. What do we mean by that? "Outside presentation" is that which affects a person's perception. It deals with how one perceives you before they even talk to you. We believe clothing, markings (tattoos) plays a major role in this. Let's make it clear, we don't believe that clothes or presentation keeps you from being saved or sends you to hell. However, we do believe that presentation can set the stage for a person to attentively receive a message from Christ. Presentation can also be used to dim your spiritual light. Jesus stated in John 7:24- Judge not according to the appearance, but judge righteous judgment. Don't do like the Pharisees did because they use to judge people *(totally formulate an opinion of a person)* by their skin, nationality, and clothing before meeting them. But Jesus also stated that you shall know them by the fruits they bare. How we present ourselves does draw or repel people. How we live can give accent to what we wear as well. A fruit grows rotten on the inside before that molding merge to the outside.

Satan's plan is to nullify us on every component of gender identification and socialization. Nevertheless, the Bible says to, "Train up a child in the way he should go and when he is old he will not depart from it."(Proverbs 22:6) I wonder what same-sex "married" couples are training the children they adopt to be or interact sexually with in same gender; especially, when they can't have children together naturally.

Presentation can solicit attention and cause a difference to be set forth at first glance, but what you do after that is on you. Remember, you got to bait a fish before you can skin it. Identification helps direct us to where we need to go to experience the desire that we seek. When we want to read a book, we look for a library. When we want to purchase a doughnut, we look for a bakery. When we want to purchase cereal with raisins, we look for "Raisin Bran".

When we want to use the bathroom, women look for the figurine with a dress and men look for the figurine with pants. However, recent news is that certain gay movements are trying to remove figurines that distinguish genders in public restrooms. In Tennessee, gay union offshoots have been striving to change parental forms to "Parent 1" and "Parent 2" in place of mother and father. It was legalized on August 21, 2015 in Tennessee. The unisex "cancer" is bleeding into every aspect of life. Remember: Song of Solomon 2:15- states: "It's the little foxes that spoil the vine." The little things that we discard as foolish, and insignificant that slowly grows into a "mountain of trouble and spiritual depletion."

We believe that these components of dress are "vital in the socialization process of raising children to formulate a mindset of gender identification and responsibility. That's why we as saints of God are identified as lights, letters, royal priesthood, and a city that set on a hill. We are the ones who form and set a precedence of how society should be and not the unbelievers. When proper presentation and socialization are in place, the gender of a man or woman does not have to be second guessed at a moment's glance. This concept certifies itself in every culture. In other words, if a woman lives in Africa, she should wear the feminine attire for African culture. This pertains to men as well. If one lives or visits Alaska, England, France, or China, this principle still holds for the outward presentation of a Christian. Presentation is one of the components used to draw others to inquire of our inner character; while our personalities, behavior, and inward qualities close the deal.

The **"Doctrine of Socialization"** is a vital doctrinal concern that deals with "conditioning the heart" to understand and believe that God is the ultimate and loving shepherd that can develop, heal, and make free any individual who will totally yield their lives to His will. Remember, even in referring to the people of God as sheep, it is not difficult to tell a "sheep" from any other animal in this world such as wolves. That's why Jesus stated to his disciples in Matthew 10:16-**Behold, I send you forth as sheep in the midst of wolves: be ye therefore wise as serpents, and harmless as doves.** Studying and mimicking the character, thinking, behavior, and commandments of

Christ is what impacts the socialization process the most and makes it work!

We believe that the "Doctrine of Presentation" is a component that deals with showing forth the characteristics and the styles externally as well as internally. It is an added benefit to the socialization process. We believe that the internal aspect of reflecting a Christ-like character is the most important because of what the bible states in 1 Samuel 16:7- But the LORD said unto Samuel, Look not on his countenance, or on the height of his stature; because I have refused him: for the LORD seeth not as man seeth; for man looketh on the outward appearance, but the LORD looketh on the heart.

However this scripture still emphasizes the truth of life that man does look on the outward appearance first when being approached by someone. That's why God had to instruct Samuel to follow His leading when choosing a King to replace Saul. God knows how man has been created to analyzed things by the outside first and that's ok because that's how God fixed our physic. He made men and women to look and act different. Just ask Adam and Eve. God knows what he's doing. That's why in the new testament Christ (God manifested in the flesh) makes it clear once again that we are living epistles <u>known</u> and <u>read</u> of men. We are a balanced force used for God to draw men to Him. It is man who we are striving to influence. That's why we are a people used to witness to men and women no matter how they may look.

DOCTRINE OF FINE ARTS, ENTERTAINMENT, AND FELLOWSHIP

Doctrine Of Fine Arts, Entertainment, And Fellowship

We believe that as people of God our entertainment, our fine arts, and our fellowship should be geared towards spiritual, morally good, clean enjoyment and praise towards God. We believe that how a believer or a group of believers (church) lives can cause their offerings, music, and praise to be rejected by God! (Amos 5:22-24)

We, at Goodness and Mercy Ministries C.A.T.B, are determined not to let that happen to us! God we need you now and always!

I. IN REGARDS TO ENTERTAINMENT-

We believe that as saints of God we should be mindful and caution ourselves not to indulge in things such as movies, music, or activities that would hinder our spiritual growth and conviction towards God. We should be sensitive not to fashion ourselves in areas according to the former lusts of our ignorance. We should strive to be holy in all manner of conversation (behavior)(1 Peter 1:14-15). We encourage the people of God to be prayerful, mindful, and guard themselves from supporting any form of entertainment that heavily promotes lifestyles that directly go against the word of God. Entertainment that promotes or encourages drug abuse, substance abuse, same-sex lifestyle, fornication, adultery, transsexualism, and violence are evil communication and should be avoided. We also warrant believers against entertainment saturated with profanity knowing that words affect the spirit of man tremendously according to the following scriptures- Colossians 3:8, Ephesians 4:29, and 2 Timothy 2:16.

II. IN REGARDS TO FINE ARTS-

Although many of us have been developed and cultivated through the schools and personal training to become adequate or professional musicians, we believed that once matured we should take these god given talents and use them to glorify His name. We believe all fine arts be it acting, dancing, or music, were created for the sole purpose to magnify God and promote His message of holiness-**Psalm 149, Psalm 150, 2 Samuel 6:16, 2 Samuel 6:14, Exodus 15:20, and Jeremiah 31:12-13.** We believe that saints of God must be careful to not indoctrinate concepts and methods of the world into the church. One example would be taking a secular song in its entirety and replacing the lyrics with gospel lyrics. The words are different, but the music is the same. This sends out a merge or mixed message to the listener.

Another thing to caution is when a secular song is used to usher in a joyful spiritual event. One song frequently played in church is "Celebrate Good Times" by Kool and the Gang.

Although this song does not promote bad lyrics, it is secular in nature and was created by a non-gospel but rhythm and blues band. Secular never adds to the spirit of God no matter what it is. Too much of it will pull away from or seduce the spirit of the event no matter how harmless it may seem to us. Remember, it's the little foxes that spoil the vine (Song of Solomon 2:15). The bible tells us in 2 Corinthians 10:4, "For the weapons of our warfare *are* not carnal, but mighty through God to the pulling down of strong holds." *(More information will be given in doctrinal class.)*

Dance is another fine art that can usher in many seducing spirits. This is why when it comes to the worship of God, we believe it is important to be prompt and led by the Holy spirit when going into a dance. Many secular dances have creeped into the churches and fostered a secular atmosphere to a HOLY GOD.

The two, gospel and worldly music, just don't mix. However, we believe what gives credence (acceptance) to a dance is the motive behind that dance. 1 Samuel 16:7 states," But the LORD said unto Samuel, Look not on his countenance, or on the height of his stature; because I have refused him: for the LORD seeth not as man seeth; for man looketh on the outward appearance, but the LORD looketh on the heart." We believe whatever dance you feel prompted to do by the spirit will not be seductive in nature, and the mindset will totally be geared on giving praise and glory to God! *(More information will be given in doctrinal class.)*

III. IN REGARDS TO FELLOWSHIP-

We believe in human fellowship. We believe that interacting with people of the same mindset in regards to growth in God is both healthy and encouraging as long as it maintains the elements of joy and without components that negatively affect the spirit of man directly such as gossiping, gluttony, illicit touching, etc.

We believe interacting with people who are not believers is not sinful as long as the believer maintains his or her spiritual principles and resides in an atmosphere that does not promote reveling, or seduction (Mark 2:13-17). Even Jesus ate with sinners. This is the perfect opportunity to be a witness for God.

We believe in total abstinence from alcohol, wine, and smoking. Although wine is mentioned as a substance used in the bible and technically not a sin, the alcoholic content in this present day wine is more potent and addictive which makes it a substance that can easily cause drunkenness. According to scripture, drunkenness is still and will always be a sin (Ephesians 5:18). On the other hand, smoking cigarettes is not an outright sin because there is no scriptural support. However, we can boldly say it is a weight. It is a weight in the sense that it can harm your body which is the temple of the Holy Ghost (1 Corinthians 6:19). The bible instructs us to lay aside every weight and the sin that so easily beset us (Hebrews 12:1). It is for this reason that at Goodness and Mercy Ministries smoking, wine or alcoholic beverages of any type are prohibited and discouraged on and off of church grounds. These components are not beneficial for believers.

CONCLUSION
THE AFFIRMATION

Conclusion

The Affirmation

We at Goodness and Mercy Ministries C.A.T.B. have accepted and embraced the fact that they that live godly will suffer persecution (2 Timothy 3:12). We were saved to live and serve out the mission of Christ. He makes it clear in Matthew 10:22, "And all nations will hate you because you are my followers. But everyone who endures to the end will be saved." Although we may suffer, we will also experience the richness, the blessings, and the abundance of the land. Jesus states in John 10:10,"The thief cometh not, but for to steal, and to kill, and to destroy: I am come that they might have life, and that they might have *it* more abundantly." Proverbs 10:22 states, "The blessing of the Lord, it maketh rich, and he addeth no sorrow with it."

While I was in my kitchen, the Lord spoke to me and said, "From the ashes of the C.A.T.B. church shall arise a holy nation that the world has not seen in decades. They will be a people who shall come forth with an anointing of God that will shake up the world in these last days. They will walk on a land of love, praying, fasting, and studying the word of God! They will not conform to the styles and antics of this nation, but will make a difference between clean and unclean and holy and unholy. I will send forth soldiers unafraid into my vineyard. I will make them a delightsome land and they will bathe in the sunlight of my blessings!

Believe prophet of God for this day and not this way.

And it shall come to pass in the last days, saith God, I will pour out of my Spirit upon all flesh: and your sons and your daughters shall prophesy, and your young men shall see visions, and your old men shall dream dreams: It will be done (Philippians 1:6)!

TO GOD BE THE GLORY!

www.ingramcontent.com/pod-product-compliance
Lightning Source LLC
Chambersburg PA
CBHW060415050426
42449CB00009B/1979